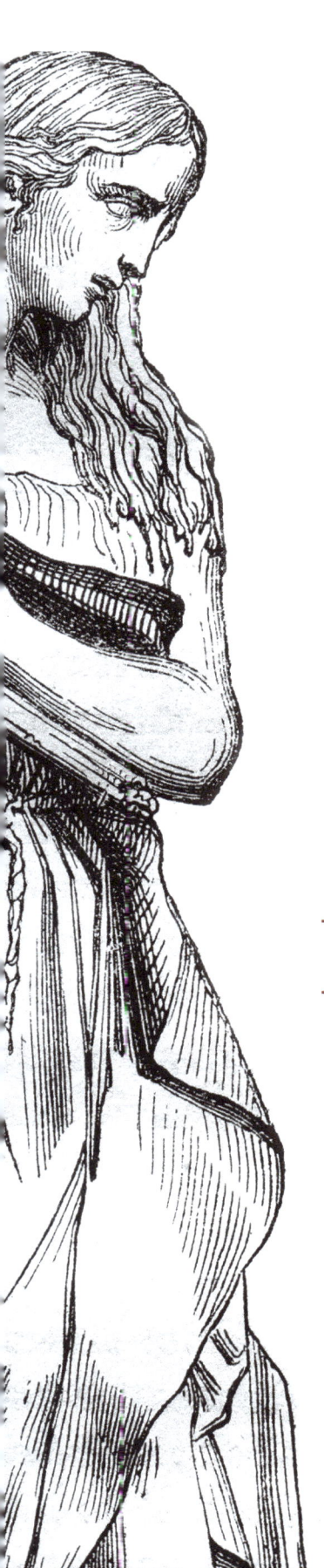

Jay Quinn

The Teachings of Mary Magdalene

Strengthening the Soul

Other Books in
The Teachings of Mary Magdalene Series

*How to Use the Inner Planes
for Transformation and Spiritual Growth*

Energetic Regeneration

Jay Quinn

The Teachings of Mary Magdalene

Strengthening the Soul

Higher Consciousness Press
Raising awareness through self mastery

Copyright © 2020 by Jay Quinn

All rights reserved. This book or any portion thereof may not be reproduced or used in any manner whatsoever without the expressed written permission of the publisher except for the use of brief quotations in a book review or scholarly journal.

First Printing: 2020

Print Book ISBN: 978-1-7343880-2-2
Ebook ISBN: 978-1-7343880-3-9

Higher Consciousness Press
4132 Conrad Road
Alexandria, Virginia 22312

www.higherconsciousnesspress.com

Book Layout ©2017 BookDesignTemplates.com
Book Cover Design by 100 Covers
Interior Formatting by FormattedBooks.com

Ordering Information:

Special discounts are available on quantity purchases by corporations, associations, educators, and others. For details, contact the publisher at the above-listed address.

U.S. trade bookstores and wholesalers: Please contact Higher Consciousness Press:
Email: higherconsciousnesspress@aol.com
www.higherconsciousnesspress.com

Dedication

*To my spiritual teacher, the Reverend Ellen Resch,
to whom I am eternally grateful for introducing me to
Spiritual Science and for believing in me before I had any clue
of my purpose and soul progression. May your soul vibration be
strengthened by the merits of the Mary Magdalene teachings.*

Contents

Acknowledgments... xi
Foreword.. xiii
Preface.. xv
Muscle Testing Disclaimer... xix

Introduction.. xxi
Requirements xxii
Mandalas.. xxiii
Removal of Imbalances on the Soul................................. xxiii
Sanctifying the Soul xxiv
Integration of the Soul Clearing Process.......................... xxiv
Validating Results Through Muscle Testing......................... xxv
Implementing the Clearing Process................................. xxv

Chapter 1: Self-Inflicted Judgments 1
Meditate on the Mandala 2
Process for Meditating on the Mandala.............................. 2
Process for Removal of Self-Inflicted Judgments 3

Chapter 2: Rejection from Others................................... 5
Meditate on the Mandala 6
Process for Meditating on the Mandala.............................. 6
Process for Removal of Rejection from Others 7

Chapter 3: Condemnation by Others.................................. 9
Meditate on the Mandala 10
Process for Meditating on the Mandala............................. 10
Process for Removal of Condemnation by Others..................... 11

Chapter 4: Denial of Your Truth by Others 13
   Meditate on the Mandala 14
   Process for Meditating on the Mandala 14
   Process for Removal of Denial of Your Truth by Others 15

Chapter 5: Communal Beliefs That Oppose Love and Light 17
   Meditate on the Mandala 18
   Process for Meditating on the Mandala 18
   Process for Removal of Communal Beliefs That Oppose Love and Light 19

Chapter 6: Self-Sabotaging Beliefs 21
   Meditate on the Mandala 22
   Process for Meditating on the Mandala 22
   Process for Removal of Self-Sabotaging Beliefs 23

Chapter 7: Bigotry 25
   Meditate on the Mandala 26
   Process for Meditating on the Mandala 26
   Process for Removal of Bigotry 27

Chapter 8: Self-Denial 29
   Meditate on the Mandala 30
   Process for Meditating on the Mandala 30
   Process for Removal Self-Denial 31

Chapter 9: The Dark Arts 33
   Meditate on the Mandala 34
   Process for Meditating on the Mandala 34
   Process for Removal of The Dark Arts 35

Chapter 10: Martyrdom 37
   Meditate on the Mandala 38
   Process for Meditating on the Mandala 38
   Process for Removal of Martyrdom 39

Chapter 11: Contracts and Vows 41

Meditate on the Mandala 42
Process for Meditating on the Mandala 42
Process for Release of Contracts and Vows 43

Chapter 12: Rejection of the Divine 45

Meditate on the Mandala 46
Process for Meditating on the Mandala 46
Process for Removal of Rejection of the Divine 47

Chapter 13: Sanctifying the Soul 49

Process for Sanctifying the Soul 50
Purifying the Soul 50
Blessing the Soul 51
Infusing Divine Love 51
Final Thoughts 52

Appendix 53

The Two-Minute Daily Medley 54
List of Illustrations 55

Glossary 57

About the Author 63

Acknowledgments

I am humbled and grateful to Mary Magdalene for selecting me to be the channel for her Inner Planes teachings.

My deepest thanks to Reverend Joseph Martinez and the other members of my healing study groups who consistently worked with the techniques and provided valuable feedback; and to Rebecca Mimms, who patiently proofed our handouts every other week and for her assistance in proofing and editing this book. Special thanks to Laurel Colless, children's environmental educator, business consultant, and author of _The Sleeping King_, for her encouragement, editing, proofing, and formatting suggestions; and to Frances Schatteman, proprietor of _The Amber Tree Inn_ in Lily Dale, New York who also provided extensive and invaluable editing and proofing assistance; and my warm gratitude to Philip Bigler, former Arlington National Cemetery Historian, 1998 National Teacher of the Year, and author of ten books, who graciously shared his experience and guidance as I began this self-publishing project. His latest book, the _Tomb of the Unknown Soldier: a Century of Honor_, is available on tomb2021.com.

Namaste, beautiful friends.

Foreword

A Message from Anna Magdalene, the grandmother of Jesus

The soul is the most precious quality that you have. It is eternal and made in the image of the Divine. The trials you have overcome and the lessons you have successfully learned strengthen your soul, while those lessons that you are still working on show you the way to reclaim your Divinity.

The Teachings of Mary Magdalene: Strengthening the Soul, and her first book, *The Teachings of Mary Magdalene: How to Use the Inner Planes for Transformation and Spiritual Growth*, provide teachings and techniques that nurture your soul and speed your journey back to the Divine.

This second book covers twelve soul imbalances or human tendencies and patterns that block soul progression. Once they are removed, your Divine expression will unfold, allowing joy and bliss to be present in your daily life.

The Magdalene lineage will support your unfoldment. Be patient. Be persistent. Be vigilant. Be Divine.

Enjoy the journey, and bring others with you.

Eternally yours,

Anna Magdalene
September 18, 2019
A channeled message to Jay Quinn

Preface

The Teachings of Mary Magdalene: Strengthening the Soul is the sequel to Mary Magdalene's initial book, *The Teachings of Mary Magdalene: How to Use the Inner Planes for Transformation and Spiritual Growth*. This second book builds on the concepts you were introduced to in her initial book and contains techniques that profoundly and deeply impact the soul.

Strengthening the Soul introduces you to twelve major soul imbalances that interfere with your soul progression and includes transformative processes for reestablishing balance and clearing the way for your soul progression. The techniques require you to work with a specific mandala for each trait and to apply the Inner Planes energies.

Prerequisites

To benefit from the transformative processes in this book, you must be familiar and adept with the major concepts explained in Mary Magdalene's first book, *The Teachings of Mary Magdalene: How to Use the Inner Planes for Transformation and Spiritual Growth*.

At the very minimum, you must have read Chapter One in Mary Magdalene's initial book and performed the prescribed tasks, including:

- ❖ Accessing the Inner Planes
- ❖ Calibrating your energy fields to the Inner Planes frequency

- ❖ Walking through the energy fields of the Masters
- ❖ Activating your Sacred Heart
- ❖ Creating the Divine Chamber

Also, you must have been working with the Inner Planes energy for at least thirty days so that your vibration is high enough to integrate the soul strengthening exercises provided in the ensuing pages. For confirmation, ask Mary Magdalene if your vibration is sufficient to proceed with the soul balancing processes.

If you are not sufficiently confident in your clairaudient skills to hear a response, you can ask "yes" and "no" questions using muscle testing to obtain an answer from Mary Magdalene. You can find a brief review of muscle testing in the Introduction to this book.

If your vibration needs to be higher, a quick and simple means of meeting that threshold is to do the eight suggested daily processes mentioned in Mary Magdalene's initial book until your vibration increases to the necessary level. Refer to The Two-Minute Daily Medley in the Appendix for a summary of the eight Inner Planes techniques suggested for daily use. Once you become familiar with the eight practices, you can do them in roughly two minutes.

If you perform the twelve soul balancing processes shown in this book while your vibration is not high enough, no harm will occur. Your energy clearing will be held in a suspended state until your vibration rises to the minimum threshold, at which time you will automatically integrate the balancing process.

Inner Plane Concepts

The Inner Plane concepts referred to in this book are introduced and explained in Mary Magdalene's first book, *The Teachings of Mary Magdalene: How to Use the Inner Planes for Transformation and Spiritual Growth*. Your familiarity, understanding, and application of these concepts are critical for successfully applying the techniques provided in this book. You can find a brief definition of the terms used in this book in the Appendix. After each term, the chapter where you can find more information in Mary Magdalene's initial book is shown in brackets.

All the material in *The Teachings of Mary Magdalene* series is channeled, as are the Foreword message by Anna Magdelene and the Final Thoughts by Mary Magdalene. I took extensive steps to ensure accuracy. You will be the final judge.

May your soul progression benefit from the miraculous teachings of Mary Magdalene.

Blessings,

Jay Quinn

Muscle Testing Disclaimer

All information, and not limited to, presented in this book is educational and provides energetic techniques to assist your transformation and spiritual growth. As part of the instruction in this book, you will be introduced to the concept of muscle testing (an intuitive communication process) to validate results and select appropriate techniques for yourself and others.

By reading this book, you understand the author or publisher does not know how you will personally respond to using muscle testing, nor can they attest to your proficiency or the accuracy of your results. You agree to accept full responsibility for any and all risks associated with using muscle testing and applying the energetic techniques shared in this book. The author and publisher accept no responsibility or liability whatsoever for the use or misuse of the information contained in this book.

The information contained in this book and the use of muscle testing is not intended to be used as a substitute for medical advice, diagnosis, or treatment. Always seek the advice of your physician or other qualified health providers for any questions you may have regarding a medical condition. Never disregard professional medical advice or delay in seeking it as a result of the contents of this book or information obtained through your muscle testing. These directions apply whether you are using muscle testing and/or the techniques in this book on yourself, another, or as a practitioner who renders services to others.

Techniques and processes contained in this book are subject to change without further notice.

Introduction

Your soul, when first created by the Divine Mind, is a replica of the Creator's Divine Essence. In a sense, you are a mini-Divine soul with all of the Divine attributes of its Creator: love, light, awareness, and free will. The Divine Mind is fully aware of being omnipresent and omnipotent. It also emanates pure love and light. Your soul must learn to develop these Divine attributes through experience and choices. This learning process generally takes your soul many lifetimes to fully embrace your Divine omniscience. The result is the reuniting of your soul with the Oneness of the Divine.

The Universal Law of Attraction (or the Law of Cause and Effect) and karma guide your evolutionary journey and are closely linked. The word "karma" comes from the Sanskrit language meaning "action – action operating through the Law of Cause and Effect."[1] Stated more simply, the karmic law says that whatever you attract in your life is a result of your previous actions. Your thoughts, words, and deeds from this and past lives plant seeds in your mind that ripen and play out over time. Similarly, the Bible states, "For whatsoever a man soweth, that shall he also reap."[2] Both the Universal Law of Attraction and the karmic law determine what you attract in your daily life and impact your experiences on a soul level.

The karmic law ensures that you receive back according to your thoughts, words, and deeds. The choices that align with your Divine Essence of pure light and

---

[1] http://dictionary.tamicube.com/sanskrit-dictionary.aspx
[2] https://www.kingjamesbibleonline.org/Bible-Verses-About-Reap-What-You-Sow; Source: King James Bible Version – Galatians 6:7

love are positive, and those that cause pain and suffering to yourself or others are negative. As the negative choices or karma build up, they attract similar situations to you.

However, you have the opportunity to choose again. This pattern repeats until you learn to be congruent with your Divine Essence and your every thought, word, and deed come from love.

When your soul awareness identifies more with your personality, you lose connection with your true Divine Awareness. And often, this leads to choices that are more ego or self-based. In this state, it is easy to be manipulated by power and control, either as the perpetrator or receiver of such behavior. Over time, it is easy to lose connection with your soul. When this occurs, one often becomes self-absorbed, materialistic at the expense of others, and disconnected with family, friends, and work associates.

This book provides a roadmap on how to become more aware of your true soul essence, how to strengthen your soul, and how to cultivate the attributes of your Divine nature. The journey is critical to your soul development. The strength of your soul affects how powerfully you show up in life and what you can accomplish. A strong soul provides groundedness in your beliefs and fortitude when confronting adversity. Having a strong soul affects every level of your being—your physical health, your emotional stability, your mental clarity, and, most importantly, the vitality of your spirit.

Requirements

Remember, as discussed in the Preface, in order to obtain the desired benefit from the exercises shown in this book, you must have performed the preliminary processes mentioned in Chapter One of Mary Magdalene's initial book, and you must have worked with the Inner Planes material for at least thirty days. An easy way to meet this criterion is to perform the eight Inner Planes techniques that Mary Magdalene suggests doing daily. See The Two-Minute Daily Medley summary in the Appendix for a quick reference of the eight daily techniques.

The strengthening of the soul exercises taught in this book require:

1. Meditating on a soul mandala for each soul imbalance for five minutes
2. Removing the soul imbalance using the Inner Planes energies
3. Completing a three-phased Sanctifying the Soul process after performing the twelve soul balancing processes

Mandalas

The word "mandala" comes from the Sanskrit language and loosely translated means "circle." Many cultures view mandalas as symbolic representations of the entire universe which influence our physical and spiritual realities.

Considering the above perspective, it is no accident that Mary Magdalene chose the word "mandalas" versus symbols or images. The mandalas, as she describes them, make the soul receptive to the releasing process across all lifetimes.

Mary Magdalene transmitted the mandalas for this book to me. The mandalas work with the energies of the Inner Planes.

Removal of Imbalances on the Soul

This book presents twelve soul imbalances that dramatically impact your soul progression and are as follows:

- Self-inflicted judgments
- Rejection from others
- Condemnation by others
- Denial of your truth by others
- Communal beliefs that oppose love and light
- Self-sabotaging beliefs
- Bigotry
- Self-denial

- ❖ The Dark Arts
- ❖ Martyrdom
- ❖ Contracts and vows
- ❖ Rejection of the Divine

These twelve soul imbalances severely hinder your soul progression because they block your connection with the Divine and prevent the transformation of your personality in each lifetime. To remove them, you can clear your soul of the twelve soul imbalances in any order, either in one sitting, or one after another over time, or however you choose. Once you remove all twelve soul traits, you will perform the Sanctifying the Soul process.

Sanctifying the Soul

You sanctify the soul in a three-phase process. First, you purify your soul with the assistance of the following Ascended Masters: Jesus, St. Germain, Hilarion, Serapis Bey, and Paul the Venetian. Second, you bless the soul using Divine Awareness. And, third, you infuse your soul with Divine Love.

Integration of the Soul Clearing Process

The integration of the soul clearing process takes two to three months to complete after you clear all twelve traits and perform the Sanctifying the Soul process. Occasionally, you may have a few soul imbalances that require repeated clearing. If so, you only need to repeat the clearing process for the particular traits followed by the three-phase Sanctifying the Soul process. You use the muscle testing process described below or your intuition to determine whether any of the soul imbalance traits need repeat clearing.

Validating Results Through Muscle Testing

Throughout this book, as in Mary Magdalene's initial book, you use muscle testing for asking questions and validating results. As a review, the muscle testing process suggested is "using your body" as a pendulum since it is an easy method to teach. To do this, either stand on the floor or sit on the edge of a chair. Straighten your spine as much as you are able without feeling any discomfort. Declare your intention that you are a clear channel for pure truth.

Instruct your trunk or upper body to move forward for a "yes" response and move backward for a "no" response when asking "yes" or "no" questions. This method of muscle testing works nicely with the Inner Planes teachings because it allows you to know whether a process is complete. This technique is what is referred to when instructed to "Use your body to muscle test."

If you are an experienced muscle tester, you certainly can use your preferred method. If muscle testing does not work for you, use your intuition, or simply trust Mary Magdalene's Inner Planes clearing process. For more information on muscle testing, refer to the Introduction in *The Teachings of Mary Magdalene: How to Use the Inner Planes for Transformation and Spiritual Growth*.

Implementing the Clearing Process

To navigate, access, and apply the energies of the Inner Planes, you use your intent. The *Merriam-Webster Dictionary* defines *intent* as "having the mind, attention, or will concentrated on something or some end or purpose."[3]

Every technique in this book provides easy-to-follow, step-by-step instructions, with the similar format as followed in the initial book: the topic name, purpose, concepts, description, and process.

---

[3] *https://www.merriam-webster.com/dictionary/intent*

In the Process section, you are directed to take certain actions such as "Go to," "Connect," "Place," "Call forth," "Enter," "Maintain," and other directive words. You perform these actions by using your intent.

The Process section also makes reference to having the Ascended Masters "intone" Divine Vibration when you are in the Temple of Spires Plane. The sound is similar to vocal overtones of the Divine Love.

CHAPTER 1

Self-Inflicted Judgments

Purpose: To remove the effects of self-inflicted judgments on the soul across all lifetimes

Concepts: Divine Chamber, Sacred Heart, the Mother, Higher Chamber Plane, Temple of Spires Plane, Divine Awareness, Ascended Masters, and Divine Vibration

Description: When you judge yourself, you leave an impression on your soul. These impressions accumulate and cause paralysis of sorts that leaves you confused. Your spirit becomes more and more removed from your true nature, causing you to feel saddened, numb, and bewildered. Self-judgments often build in intensity and carry over from one lifetime to another, dimming the vitality of your soul.

The clearing process is performed three times—once for thoughts, a second time for spoken words, and a final time for deeds.

Meditate on the Mandala

Self-Inflicted Judgments

Process for Meditating on the Mandala

- ❖ Go to the Divine Chamber.
- ❖ Connect with your Sacred Heart.
- ❖ Ask the Mother to clear your mind.
- ❖ Connect with all your self-inflicted judgments in any lifetime.
- ❖ Focus on the mandala for five minutes. Concentrate on the dot in the center.
- ❖ Use your body to muscle test that the process is complete.

Process for Removal of Self-Inflicted Judgments

- Go to the Higher Chamber Plane.
- See the lightning in the sky strike the space in front of you, creating a charged sphere.
- Step into the sphere and remain until the shifting is complete.
- Go to the Temple of Spires Plane and ask the Ascended Masters to intone Divine Vibration into your soul.
- Go to the Divine Chamber.
- Connect to all your self-inflicted judgments in the form of thoughts across all your lifetimes and place Divine Awareness over them.
- Hold until all self-inflicted judgments of thoughts clear.
- Repeat the above process for verbalized self-inflicted judgments.
- Repeat the above process for all self-inflicted judgments in the form of deeds.
- Use your body to muscle test that the process is complete.

CHAPTER 2

Rejection from Others

Purpose: To remove the effects of rejection from others on the soul across all lifetimes

Concepts: Divine Chamber, Sacred Heart, the Mother, Higher Chamber Plane, Divine Awareness, Temple of Spires Plane, Ascended Masters, Divine Vibration, Oosaram Location, and Ascended Masters Plane

Description: When you experience rejection from others, the offender is generally coming from power, control, and manipulation, and projects his/her shortcomings onto you. The encounter causes you to experience pain, your heart chakra constricts, and you lose connection to those around you. The rejection causes you to deny your Divinity and creates feelings of isolation and abandonment. Of course, these feelings are illusions, making you feel separate. These misperceptions cause you to identify with your personality rather than the true essence of your soul.

These rejections poison the soul and cause it to recoil. The vibration of rejection from others remains imbedded on the soul, and the memory of that can carry over from lifetime to lifetime. The more frequently you experience rejection, the harder it is to connect to your Divinity.

Meditate on the Mandala

Rejection from Others

Process for Meditating on the Mandala

- ❖ Go to the Divine Chamber.
- ❖ Connect with your Sacred Heart.
- ❖ Ask the Mother to clear your mind.
- ❖ Connect with all situations where you experienced rejection from others in any lifetime.
- ❖ Focus on the mandala for five minutes. Concentrate on the dot in the center.
- ❖ Use your body to muscle test that the process is complete.

Process for Removal of Rejection from Others

- ❖ Go to the Higher Chamber Plane.
- ❖ Connect to all the times that you have experienced rejection from others in any lifetime.
- ❖ Neutralize the feelings of rejection by overlaying Divine Awareness over each situation.
- ❖ Go to the Temple of Spires Plane and ask the Ascended Masters to intone your soul with Divine Vibration.
- ❖ Go to the Oosaram location in the Ascended Masters Plane.
- ❖ Remain five seconds or longer until your soul vibration rises.
- ❖ Use your body to muscle test that the process is complete.

CHAPTER 3

Condemnation by Others

Purpose: To remove the effects of condemnation by others on the soul across all lifetimes

Concepts: Divine Chamber, Sacred Heart, the Mother, Ascended Masters Plane, Temple of Spires Plane, Ascended Masters, Divine Vibration, Divine Awareness, and Divine Frequency

Description: By condemnation of others, we are referring to any situation that produces shame, guilt, and isolation.

Condemnation by others is very damaging to the soul. It causes you to constrict, lose self-confidence, and restrains the development of your soul. When this occurs, it could take several lifetimes to recover.

Meditate on the Mandala

Condemnation by Others

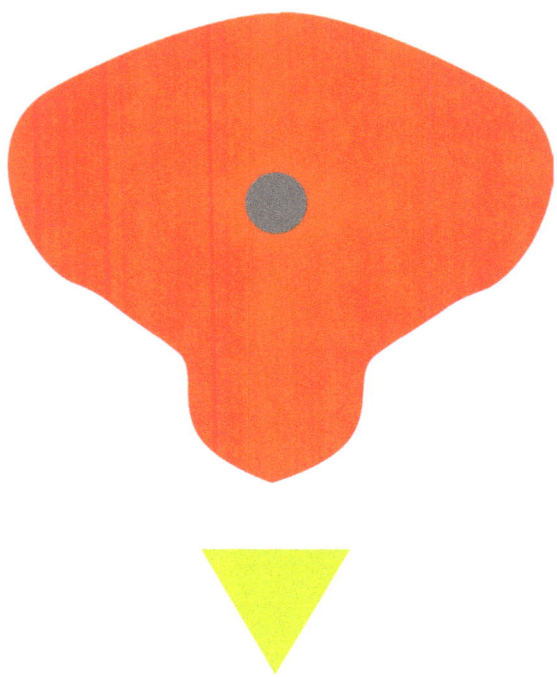

Process for Meditating on the Mandala

- ❖ Go to the Divine Chamber.
- ❖ Connect with your Sacred Heart.
- ❖ Ask the Mother to clear your mind.
- ❖ Connect with all situations where you have experienced condemnation by others and felt shame, guilt, and isolation in any lifetime.
- ❖ Focus on the mandala for five minutes. Concentrate on the dot in the center.
- ❖ Use your body to muscle test that the process is complete.

Process for Removal of Condemnation by Others

- Go to the Ascended Masters Plane.
- Connect to all the times that you have experienced condemnation by others in any lifetime.
- Upon seeing three orb-like spheres, allow them to clear your field.
- Go to the Temple of Spires Plane and have the Ascended Masters intone your soul with Divine Vibration.
- Connect with all your lifetimes and place Divine Awareness over your soul in each lifetime.
- Hold until all condemnation vibrations release.
- Have the Divine Frequency restore your soul to its original, pure state.
- Use your body to muscle test that the process is complete.

CHAPTER 4

Denial of Your Truth by Others

Purpose: To remove the effects of denial of your truth by others across all lifetimes

Concepts: Divine Chamber, Sacred Heart, the Mother, and Divine Awareness

Description: Denial of your truth by others generally occurs from authority figures such as your parents, teachers, religious leaders, or occupational professionals. These denials dim your light and imbed the other person's truth into your soul. These intrusions cause discordance, confusion, and interference on a very deep level. When you connect to these violations, either consciously or unconsciously, you connect to the other person's soul, and you cause interference in his/her soul with your thoughts and feelings.

The denial of your truth by others is corrected by neutralizing or balancing their "truth" affecting your soul and by balancing the interference you caused on their souls with your thoughts and feelings. In this way, both parties find inner peace.

Meditate on the Mandala

Denial of Your Truth by Others

Process for Meditating on the Mandala

- ❖ Go to the Divine Chamber.
- ❖ Connect with your Sacred Heart.
- ❖ Ask the Mother to clear your mind.
- ❖ Connect with all situations where you experienced denial of your truth by others in any lifetime.
- ❖ Focus on the mandala for five minutes. Concentrate on the dot in the center.
- ❖ Use your body to muscle test that the process is complete.

Process for Removal of Denial of Your Truth by Others

- Go to the Divine Chamber.
- Connect to the incidences in all of your lifetimes where those in authority denied your truth.
- Place Divine Awareness over all of those situations in any of your lifetimes.
- Continue to hold Divine Awareness until all denial vibrations transmute.
- Now place Divine Awareness over the souls of those who denied your truth and let it balance your feelings and thoughts that interfere with their soul vibration.
- Use your body to muscle test that the process is complete.

CHAPTER 5

Communal Beliefs That Oppose Love and Light

Purpose: To remove the effects of communal beliefs that oppose love and light on the soul across all lifetimes

Concepts: Divine Chamber, Sacred Heart, the Mother, Divine Awareness, Temple of Spires, Ascended Masters, Divine Vibration, Higher Chamber Plane, Heart Chakra, and Sixth Chakra

Description: Communal beliefs that oppose love and light are harder to detect because they are societal beliefs and because they are all your outer personality knows. It is only with great discernment that one generally has conscious awareness of these beliefs. Being societal beliefs, they are in play for your entire lifetime and become an always present way of being. Even with awareness, you are operating on two standards: what society requires and what your awakened soul needs. Even if you are aware of them, these ever-present beliefs dull the soul.

And because the beliefs are untrue, they create a cloud-like denseness over your soul. This barrier makes it difficult for your soul essence, or Divine Vibration, to shine through in your everyday activities. As a result, you feel disconnected, aimless, and lost.

Meditate on the Mandala

Communal Beliefs that Oppose Love and Light

Process for Meditating on the Mandala

- ❖ Go to the Divine Chamber.
- ❖ Connect with your Sacred Heart.
- ❖ Ask the Mother to clear your mind.
- ❖ Connect with all situations where communal beliefs opposed love and light in any lifetime.
- ❖ Focus on the mandala for five minutes. Concentrate on the dot in the center.
- ❖ Use your body to muscle test that the process is complete.

Process for Removal of Communal Beliefs That Oppose Love and Light

- Go to the Divine Chamber.
- Place Divine Awareness over the communal beliefs that oppose love and light in any lifetime.
- Hold the connection until the beliefs are neutralized or balanced.
- Go to the Temple of Spires Plane and ask the Ascended Masters to intone Divine Vibration into your soul.
- Go to the Higher Chamber Plane.
- See in the distance a star in the night sky. Feel a beam of light coming from the star shining on your heart chakra, providing the truth relative to the communal beliefs.
- When that process is complete, see the beam shine on your sixth chakra, providing understanding relative to the untruths of the communal beliefs.
- Use your body to muscle test that the process is complete.

CHAPTER 6

Self-Sabotaging Beliefs

Purpose: To remove the effects of self-sabotaging beliefs on the soul across all lifetimes

Concepts: Divine Chamber, Sacred Heart, the Mother, Divine Awareness, Temple of Spires, Ascended Masters, Divine Vibration, Higher Chamber Plane, and the Father

Description: Self-sabotaging beliefs, by their very nature, are self-created and are caused by feelings of unworthiness and guilt. They prevent the self-nurturing nature of the universe from supporting your needs. This ever-present force of the universe supports the fulfillment of your desires. If you have unworthiness in your desires, it will attract those types of situations and cause a downward, self-defeating spiral. These experiences are very painful for you and those connected to you. The beliefs get imbedded in the soul and are difficult to shift without assistance. The soul carries these feelings of unworthiness from one lifetime to another. These self-sabotaging patterns require a deep inner focus and spiritual strength to shift and generally require several lifetimes to resolve.

The following balancing process clears the soul of the unworthiness vibration immediately so that it does not take you multiple lifetimes to correct.

Meditate on the Mandala

Self-Sabotage

Process for Meditating on the Mandala

- ❖ Go to the Divine Chamber.
- ❖ Connect with your Sacred Heart.
- ❖ Ask the Mother to clear your mind.
- ❖ Connect with all experiences of self-sabotage in any lifetime.
- ❖ Focus on the mandala for five minutes. Concentrate on the dot in the center.
- ❖ Use your body to muscle test that the process is complete.

Process for Removal of Self-Sabotaging Beliefs

- ❖ Go to the Divine Chamber.
- ❖ Place Divine Awareness over the self-sabotaging thoughts, words, and deeds in any lifetime. Hold the connection until the beliefs are neutralized or balanced.
- ❖ Go to the Temple of Spires Plane and ask the Ascended Masters to intone Divine Vibration into your soul.
- ❖ Go to the Higher Chamber Plane and ask the Mother to remove the pattern from each lifetime.
- ❖ Ask the Father to provide the truth of each occurrence.
- ❖ Use your body to muscle test that the process is complete.

CHAPTER 7

Bigotry

Purpose: To remove the effects of bigotry on the soul across all lifetimes

Concepts: Divine Chamber, Sacred Heart, the Mother, Divine Awareness, Temple of Spires, Ascended Master, Divine Vibration, Higher Chamber Plane, and the Father

Description: Bigotry is poison to the soul. It violates the sanctity of the soul on many levels. Bigoted thoughts, words, or deeds destroy the Divine connection with self and others. It fosters hatred. It separates and raises your self-worth above others. And, when done by those in authority, bigotry is wielded as a weapon for power and control and easily influences those around them by either encouraging similar behavior from others or causing people to recoil and do nothing, splintering their souls.

Bigotry overshadows love and light, driving you further away from your Divinity.

Meditate on the Mandala

Bigotry

Process for Meditating on the Mandala

- ❖ Go to the Divine Chamber.
- ❖ Connect with your Sacred Heart.
- ❖ Ask the Mother to clear your mind.
- ❖ Connect with all situations where you experienced bigotry or where you acted as the perpetrator of bigotry in any lifetime.
- ❖ Focus on the mandala for five minutes. Concentrate on the dot in the center.
- ❖ Use your body to muscle test that the process is complete.

Process for Removal of Bigotry

- Go to the Divine Chamber.
- Connect with your Sacred Heart and ask the Mother to clear your mind.
- Place Divine Awareness over all bigotry you have experienced or perpetrated in the form of thoughts, words, and deeds in any lifetime.
- Hold the connection until the balancing is complete.
- Go to the Temple of Spires Plane and ask the Ascended Masters to intone Divine Vibration into your soul.
- Go to the Higher Chamber Plane and ask the Mother to remove the pattern from each lifetime.
- Ask the Father to replace the bigotry patterns with the appropriate qualities for each situation.
- Use your body to muscle test that the process is complete.

CHAPTER 8

Self-Denial

Purpose: To remove the effects of self-denial on the soul across all lifetimes

Concepts: Divine Chamber, Sacred Heart, the Mother, Divine Awareness, and the Father

Description: Self-denial cuts you off from the Divine and drains your soul energy. It prevents the revitalization of the soul, leaving the soul depleted and flat.

As with self-sabotaging beliefs, when you deny yourself, you prevent the supportive nature of the universe from nurturing you. You withdraw within yourself, unable to accept nurturance from those around you. Also, you lose the will to do those things that you know will nurture yourself. Moreover, self-denial restricts the flow of the Divine through you, making it difficult for you to be an instrument of the Divine for good in the Universe.

Self-denial also prevents you from being able to be compassionately present for another. It blocks you from being your true authentic self.

And in this state, it is easy to lose connection to your purpose in life and the lessons your soul intended to learn. The antidote for self-denial is self-love. Love exists within you, those around you, and the Universe. Reconnecting to these sources of love restores the soul..

Meditate on the Mandala

Self-Denial

Process for Meditating on the Mandala

- ❖ Go to the Divine Chamber.
- ❖ Connect with your Sacred Heart.
- ❖ Ask the Mother to clear your mind.
- ❖ Connect with all occasions where you experienced self-denial in any lifetime.
- ❖ Focus on the mandala for five minutes. Concentrate on the dot in the center.
- ❖ Use your body to muscle test that the process is complete.

Process for Removal Self-Denial

- ❖ Go to the Divine Chamber.
- ❖ Place Divine Awareness over all the self-denial occasions in any lifetime.
- ❖ Hold the connection until all self-denial aspects of yourself are balanced.
- ❖ Ask the Mother to remove the pattern of self-denial from all lifetimes.
- ❖ Ask the Father to replace the patterns with self-love.
- ❖ Use your body to muscle test that the process is complete.

CHAPTER 9

The Dark Arts

Purpose: To remove the effects of the dark arts on the soul across all lifetimes

Concepts: Divine Chamber, Sacred Heart, the Mother, Divine Awareness, Temple of Spires Plane, Ascended Masters, Divine Vibration, Higher Chamber Plane, and the Father

Description: Dark arts are modalities that use energy, either intentionally or sometimes unintentionally, to harm others. Using dark arts such as curses, hexes, spells, black magic, etc., is destructive to the soul. It blocks light and access to higher vibrations. It makes you more easily accessible to the dark, which becomes attracted to you and makes you a vehicle for their ends, promising power, control, and fortune. The negative forces infiltrate the soul and eventually consume your soul to such an extent that it is nearly impossible to regain access to your light without Divine intervention. Avoid this path at all costs.

Meditate on the Mandala

The Dark Arts

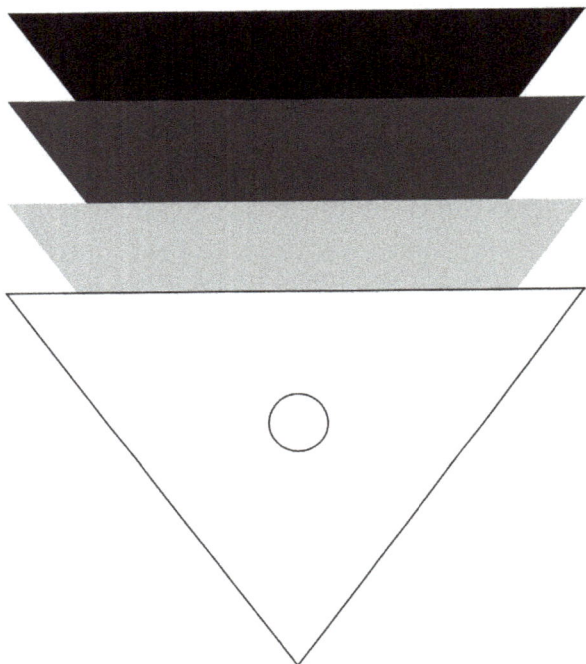

Process for Meditating on the Mandala

- ❖ Go to the Divine Chamber.
- ❖ Connect with your Sacred Heart.
- ❖ Ask the Mother to clear your mind.
- ❖ Connect with all lifetimes where you practiced the dark arts.
- ❖ Focus on the mandala for five minutes. Concentrate on the dot in the center.
- ❖ Use your body to muscle test that the process is complete.

Process for Removal of The Dark Arts

- Go to the Divine Chamber.
- See a laser beam of Divine light.
- Direct the beam at the darkness of your soul caused by the use of the dark arts in any lifetime.
- Maintain connection until the darkness breaks up and dissolves and you can see a white dot of light.
- Place Divine Awareness over each situation in which you used the dark arts in any lifetime.
- Hold the connection with the Divine Awareness until the soul transforms into pure white light.
- Go to the Temple of Spires Plane and ask the Ascended Masters to intone your soul with Divine Vibration.
- Go to the Higher Chamber Plane and ask the Mother to remove the patterns of dark art usage across all lifetimes.
- Ask the Father to replace the patterns with Divine understanding and compassion for yourself and the others involved.
- Use your body to muscle test that the process is complete.

CHAPTER 10

Martyrdom

Purpose: To remove the effects of martyrdom on the soul across all lifetimes

Concepts: Divine Chamber, Sacred Heart, the Mother, Divine Awareness, Temple of Spires Plane, Ascended Masters, and Divine Vibration

Description: Martyrdom has an interesting vibration. On one hand, you make a stand for the light and higher principles and, on the other, the resultant painful and public humiliation leaves you feeling more like a victim and abandoned by the Divine.

The experience of martyrdom leaves a very strong and deep impression on the soul. The memory is painful and blocks the connection to your Divine Essence. On a practical level, it impacts your ability to take a stand for justice in all succeeding lifetimes. When called to take a stand, you connect to the pain on some level, which causes paralysis, indecision, and despair.

Meditate on the Mandala

Martyrdom

Process for Meditating on the Mandala

- ❖ Go to the Divine Chamber.
- ❖ Connect with your Sacred Heart.
- ❖ Ask the Mother to clear your mind.
- ❖ Connect to all lifetimes where you experienced martyrdom.
- ❖ Focus on the mandala for five minutes. Concentrate on the dot in the center.
- ❖ Use your body to muscle test that the process is complete.

Process for Removal of Martyrdom

- Go to the Divine Chamber.
- Place Divine Awareness over each lifetime of martyrdom.
- Extend the Divine Awareness out to include all those involved—directly or indirectly.
- Hold the Divine Awareness connection until there is a release or a feeling of neutrality.
- Go to the Temple of Spires Plane and ask the Ascended Masters to intone your soul with Divine Vibration.
- Use your body to muscle test that the process is complete.

CHAPTER 11

Contracts and Vows

Purpose: To remove the effects of contracts and vows on the soul across all lifetimes

Concepts: Divine Chamber, Sacred Heart, the Mother, Divine Vibration, Temple of Spires, and Ascended Masters

Description: Contracts and vows leave an impression on the soul. They influence all succeeding lifetimes in some way, depending on the severity of the situations. The soul records not only all the contracts and vows but also all occasions of broken contracts and vows. The reactions of people to situations around contracts and vows are generally severe and are either positive or negative, depending on the circumstances. When meeting parties involved in contracts or vows from past lifetimes in this lifetime, you may feel either a strong attraction or repulsion either to those parties or to similar commitment encounters.

Any past altercations can cause paralysis, indecision, mistrust, anger, violence, a sense of abandonment or rejection, or even a loss of self in this current lifetime.

Meditate on the Mandala

Contracts and Vows

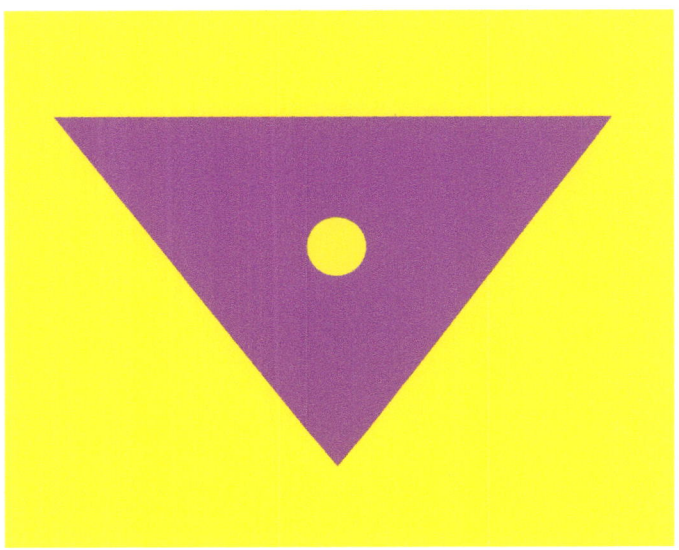

Process for Meditating on the Mandala

- ❖ Go to the Divine Chamber.
- ❖ Connect with your Sacred Heart.
- ❖ Ask the Mother to clear your mind.
- ❖ Connect with all situations involving contracts and vows in any lifetime.
- ❖ Focus on the mandala for five minutes. Concentrate on the dot in the center.
- ❖ Use your body to muscle test that the process is complete.

Process for Release of Contracts and Vows

- Go to the Divine Chamber.
- Connect to all lifetimes where there are contracts and vows.
- See a sun disk of Divine Vibration and then overlay the Divine Vibration over each contract or vow made in any lifetime, using your intent.
- Extend the Divine Vibration to include all parties involved and dissolve the energy of the contracts and vows.
- Go to the Temple of Spires Plane and ask the Ascended Masters to intone your soul with Divine Vibration until all traces of contracts and vows are completely balanced.
- Use your body to muscle test that the process is complete.

CHAPTER 12

Rejection of the Divine

Purpose: To remove the effects of rejection of the Divine on the soul across all lifetimes

Concepts: Divine Chamber, Sacred Heart, the Mother, Divine Awareness, the Father, Temple of Spires, Ascended Masters, and Divine Vibration

Description: Rejection of the Divine is very serious because you are rejecting your Creator and your Divinity. The projection causes a split on a soul level resulting in a loss of self, leading you to drift aimlessly, feel disconnected from self and others, experience deep sorrow, and have strong feelings of meaninglessness.

The split on a soul level stops your spiritual progression. The inner compass that draws you home to the Divine is missing, thus causing you to feel lost, disconnected from any sense of community, religious or otherwise, and even from your immediate family.

Meditate on the Mandala

Rejection of the Divine

Process for Meditating on the Mandala

- ❖ Go to the Divine Chamber.
- ❖ Connect with your Sacred Heart.
- ❖ Ask the Mother to clear your mind.
- ❖ Connect with all situations where you rejected the Divine in any lifetime.
- ❖ Focus on the mandala for five minutes. Concentrate on the dot in the center.
- ❖ Use your body to muscle test that the process is complete.

Process for Removal of Rejection of the Divine

- ❖ Go to the Divine Chamber.
- ❖ Place Divine Awareness over every lifetime where the rejection of the Divine took place.
- ❖ Ask the Father energy to provide the correct understanding of each situation.
- ❖ Go to the Temple of Spires Plane and ask the Ascended Masters to intone Divine Vibration into your soul and each occurrence until you remove all traces of rejection of the Divine.
- ❖ Use your body to muscle test that the process is complete.

CHAPTER 13

Sanctifying the Soul

Purpose: To purify, bless, and infuse Divine Love into the soul after clearing the twelve imbalances

Concepts: Divine Chamber, Divine Awareness, Ascended Masters Jesus, St. Germain, Hilarion, Serapis Bey, and Paul the Venetian, Sacred Heart, and Divine Love

Description: After you clear the twelve imbalances, you sanctify the soul in a three-phase process. First, you purify your soul with the assistance of the Ascended Masters Jesus, St. Germain, Hilarion, Serapis Bey, and Paul the Venetian. Second, you bless your soul using Divine Awareness. And third, you infuse your soul with Divine Love.

Occasionally, you may need to repeat the clearing process for one or more soul imbalances. If this is necessary, you repeat the soul balancing process only for those specific traits requiring additional clearing and then repeat the Sanctifying the Soul process.

The Sanctifying the Soul process cleanses the soul of impurities of the heart. By this expression, we are referring to the "ignorance" of human choices.

The purification process facilitates a more vibrant expression of your Divine Essence. Your will, awareness, and clarity of mind strengthen. Creation and manifestation of what you need naturally occur. Your daily life will have a greater sense of ease and flow.

The blessing of your soul generates greater awareness of your purpose and role in the Universe.

The infusion of Divine Love brightens your soul and enhances your awareness of being a vehicle for Divine expression in the world.

The integration of the soul clearing process takes two to three months to complete after you clear all twelve traits and perform the Sanctifying the Soul process.

Process for Sanctifying the Soul

Purifying the Soul

- ❖ Go to the Divine Chamber.
- ❖ Connect with Divine Awareness.
- ❖ Call forth Ascended Masters Jesus, St. Germain, Hilarion, Serapis Bey, and Paul the Venetian.
- ❖ The Ascended Masters sit in a circle to form a circular pool of golden Divine energy.
- ❖ Insert your soul into the pool of golden Divine energy for purification.
- ❖ Use your body to muscle test to confirm that the process is complete.

Blessing the Soul

- ❖ Go to the Divine Chamber.
- ❖ Connect to your Sacred Heart.
- ❖ Ask the Divine Awareness to bless your soul.
- ❖ Use your body to muscle test to confirm that the process is complete.

Infusing Divine Love

- ❖ Go to the Divine Chamber.
- ❖ Proceed to the back of the chamber.
- ❖ See a sun-like sphere of pulsating Divine Love.
- ❖ Place your soul in front of the pulsating Divine Love.
- ❖ The pulsating Divine Love strengthens the Divine Love within you. This strengthening will be permanent.
- ❖ Stay only for a short period, long enough to absorb the portion of Divine Love that your soul can process at this visit (two or three minutes at most).
- ❖ Use your body to muscle test to confirm that the process is complete.

Wait at least two days before absorbing another infusion of Divine Love. Repeat this process every couple of days until your soul can tolerate the full infusion of Divine Love. Use your intuition and muscle testing to guide you through the infusion process.

Final Thoughts

by Mary Magdalene

The soul expresses who you are and what you will become. Your soul has depth and richness. It is a reflection of your inner work and spiritual growth.

Your outer world and what you attract to you match the attention that you have paid to your soul. The vitality of your soul has a direct correlation to the choices you make and the dedication you make to your spiritual growth.

My first book, *The Teachings of Mary Magdalene: How to Use the Inner Planes for Transformation and Spiritual Growth,* prepared you for the soul sanctification process that you performed with this second book after clearing the twelve soul imbalances. The purification process catapults your transformation. Your Divinity can now shine forth, and you can more potently contribute to the raising of human consciousness on Planet Earth.

The third book in the series focuses on energetic regeneration and builds on the teachings of my first two books. To benefit fully from the energetic regeneration process, those interested must have a working knowledge of the Inner Planes and have performed the daily exercises introduced in the initial book for at least thirty days, as well as have completed the Strengthening the Soul exercises, and the Sanctifying the Soul processes shared in this second book.

The teachings of the third book are truly revolutionary in shifting paradigms around aging and cellular health. I invite you to continue your journey with me and learn how to use the Inner Planes energies to increase your longevity and physical health.

Sending you much love and blessings from myself and the Magdalene lineage.

Mary Magdalene
September 18, 2019
A channeled message to Jay Quinn

Appendix

The Two-Minute Daily Medley

A collection of Mary Magdalene practices suggested for daily use

Maintaining Balance
- Go to the Higher Chamber Plane.
- Ask the Father and Mother to restore balance.

Learning How to Pray
- Go to the Higher Chamber Plane.
- Ask the Mother to clear your mind.
- Ask your Sacred Heart to request what your Higher Self needs.

Raising the Soul Vibration
- Go to the Oosaram location in the Higher Chamber Plane.
- Remain until your soul is balanced and your vibration is raised.

Strengthening the Soul
- Go to the Higher Chamber Plane.
- Summon the Father and Mother energies and ask them to strengthen your soul.

Healing Physical Conditions
- Go to the Higher Chamber Plane.
- Ask the Mother and Father energies to balance your energy.
- Call forth the appropriate Ascended Masters to treat all the conditions at the same time.
- Hold the connection until complete.

Going to the Healing Room for Healing
- Go to the Healing Room in the Ascended Masters Plane.
- Allow the Ascended Masters to work on whatever needs healing.

Cultivating Joy in Your Life
- Go to the center of the Temple of Spires.
- Stand under the dome-like structure.

- Feel the energy of the Temple of Spires rise through your feet and proceed up to your head.
- Once the energy reaches your head, see golden energy shower down over you.
- When it reaches your soul center, the energy expands out from the soul center in all directions.
- Remain under the dome replenishing your joy until complete.

Connecting to Source
- Go to the Higher Chamber Plane
- Call forth the Father and Mother energies and ask them to prepare your Heart Chakra.
- Go to the Temple of Spires Plane and ask the Ascended Masters to intone Divine Vibration into your Heart Chakra.
- Then go to the Ascended Masters Plane. Observe the sun-like image in the sky and ask it to connect you to Source.

List of Illustrations

Mandalas

Self-Inflicted Judgments	Chapter 1
Rejection from Others	Chapter 2
Condemnation by Others	Chapter 3
Denial of Your Truth by Others	Chapter 4
Communal Beliefs That Oppose Love and Light	Chapter 5
Self-Sabotaging Beliefs	Chapter 6
Bigotry	Chapter 7
Self-Denial	Chapter 8
The Dark Arts	Chapter 9
Martyrdom	Chapter 10
Contracts and Vows	Chapter 11
Rejection of the Divine	Chapter 12
The Two-Minute Daily Medley	Appendix

Glossary

The following list of terms summarizes the Inner Planes concepts used in this book. In brackets after each definition is the chapter number in the initial book (The Teachings of Mary Magdalene: How to Use the Inner Planes for Transformation and Spiritual Growth) where you can find more detailed information on each concept.

Ascended Masters - Enlightened beings dedicated to helping the soul progression of ascending beings. The Ascended Masters shift vibration and increase the consciousness of other ascending beings throughout the universe according to their assigned tasks within the Divine Mind. They provide enlightened activities throughout all three Inner Planes, including the nine planes of existence within the Higher Chamber Plane. [Chapter 1, Inner Planes]

Ascended Masters Plane - One of the three primary planes within the Inner Planes. The two thousand Ascended Masters who reside in the Ascended Masters Plane use specific areas within the Ascended Masters Plane for physical, emotional, and mental balancing. [Chapter 1, Inner Planes]

Awareness - The part of you that witnesses, observes, and knows that you are a separate and distinct entity in the universe and discerns that you are more than your body. [Chapter 6, Shifting Reality]

Divine Awareness - Divine Awareness is the consciousness within the Divine Mind, and it has a balancing effect on all of creation. On a more individual basis,

Divine Awareness, when focused on imbalances across all your lifetimes, restores balance. [Chapter 7, Accessing Divine Awareness]

Divine Chamber - The Divine Chamber is a space within the Inner Planes used for connecting to the Divine Mind and Divine Awareness. It is created within the Inner Planes by integrating aspects of the Ascended Masters, Temple of Spires, and Higher Chamber Inner Planes. When working within the Divine Chamber, your mind and the Divine Mind are one. [Chapter 1, Inner Planes]

Divine Essence - Divine Essense exists in beings endowed with all the abilities of the Creator, having awareness and the ability to choose. Humans and other beings with Divine Essence can create, manifest, and connect to "All That Is." [Chapter 2, Increasing Spirituality]

Divine Frequency - Divine Frequency is a resonance, similar to overtones, and is constantly broadcast throughout the day and throughout the universe by Ascended Masters from the Temple of Spires Plane. [Chapter 6, Shifting Reality]

Divine Mind - The mind of the Creator from which all things are created and nurtured. [Chapter 1, Inner Planes, & Chapter 5, Developing Metaphysical Skills]

Divine Vibration - Divine Vibration exists in all of creation, and when connecting on this level, you are one with "All That Is." You use intent to connect to all your lifetimes through Divine Vibration. [Chapter 6, Shifting Reality]

Father - The Father energy is the Divine Masculine intelligence within the Inner Planes used for balancing and infusing the correct understanding and qualities across all lifetimes. [Chapter 1, Inner Planes]

Heart Chakra - The Heart Chakra is an energy center located in the middle of the chest and is one of twelve chakras or energy centers that allow life force to flow into the physical body to keep you vibrant and healthy. The heart chakra, or fourth chakra, bridges the lower chakras of matter and the upper chakras of spirit and connects your body, mind, emotions, and spirit. The heart chakra is your source of love and connection to others. [Chapter 4, Healing Techniques]

Higher Chamber Plane - The Higher Chamber Plane contains all of creation and, from within this space, you can shift reality and elevate mental and spiritual consciousness. The Higher Chamber Plane impacts consciousness on a soul level and affects all lifetimes.

The Higher Chamber Plane contains the consciousness of the Divine Masculine and the Divine Feminine (commonly referred to as the Father and Mother energies) that pervades all of creation and maintains the delicate balance of the universe. The Higher Chamber Plane orchestrates the mystical influences of the heavenly bodies, the application of Universal Laws, and the synchronistic movement of the universe. Nine planes of existence dwell within the Higher Chamber Plane. [Chapter 1, Inner Planes]

Inner Planes - The Inner Planes is a state of consciousness that contains and maintains all of creation. It exists within the Divine Mind in a non-physical form and ensures the nurturing and sustaining qualities of Divine Awareness, which permeate all of creation.[Introduction and Chapter 1, Inner Planes]

Intent - The use of your mind, attention, or will for a particular purpose to navigate the Inner Planes and execute actions within the Inner Planes. [Introduction]

Issues - Issues are unhealed aspects from this or past lives that hinder your spiritual development. [Introduction]

Karma - A consequence of the Universal Law of Cause and Effect which demonstrates that whatever you send into the universe comes back to you. The Law of Cause and Effect is a way in which the Universe or the Divine Mind attracts similar situations to you allowing you more opportunity to learn and make better choices. [Chapter 2, Increasing Spirituality]

Law of Attraction - A universal law that attracts circumstances and situations to you for your soul growth. [Chapter 3, Discerning Truth]

Mandala - The word "mandala" comes from the Sanskrit language and loosely translated means "circle." Many cultures view mandalas as symbolic representations of the entire universe which influence our physical and spiritual realities. [Introduction of this book]

Mother - The Mother energy is the Divine Feminine intelligence within the Inner Planes used for balancing and transforming patterns across all lifetimes. [Chapter 1, Inner Planes]

Muscle Testing - Muscle testing allows tapping into your innate intelligence, higher self, and the Magdalene lineage to obtain information not otherwise available to the conscious mind. When you ask "yes" and "no" questions, muscle testing enables you to select the best techniques and move through the processes confidently. [Chapter 1, Inner Planes]

Oosaram Location - A location in the Ascended Masters Plane used to raise your soul vibration. [Chapter 2, Increasing Spirituality]

Sacred Heart - The Sacred Heart contains your eternal flame, which is activated within the Inner Planes by the Divine Masculine and Feminine energies. Once activated, it can never be put out. It contains the purity of Divine Love. [Chapter 1, Inner Planes]

Sanctifying the Soul Process - The process applied after you clear the twelve soul imbalances in a three-phase process. First, you purify your soul with the assistance of the Ascended Masters Jesus, St. Germain, Hilarion, Serapis Bey, and Paul the Venetian. Second, you bless your soul using Divine Awareness. And third, you infuse your soul with Divine Love. [Chapter 13, Sanctifying the Soul in this book]

Sixth Chakra - One of twelve chakras or energy centers that allow life force to flow into the physical body. This chakra is located between the eyebrows. It is also referred to as the "third eye" chakra and is your energy center of intuition. [Chapter 1, Inner Planes]

Soul - The soul is the Creator's experience as you over all your lifetimes. It holds the memory of all your experiences. The soul gives rise to spirit. Once incarnated in physical form, the soul gradually develops an ego which is necessary to flourish on the Earth Plane.

The soul is Divine Essence. Divine Essence exists in beings endowed with all the abilities of the Creator—having awareness, and the ability to choose. Humans and other beings with Divine Essence can create, manifest, and connect to "All That Is." [Chapter 2, Increasing Spirituality, and Chapter 4, Healing Techniques]

Temple of Spires Plane - One of the three primary planes in the Inner Planes whose main purpose is to magnify Divine Vibration and to broadcast Divine frequencies throughout the Universe. The four corners of the Temple of Spires have spires that ascend 400 feet high and act much like broadcasting or cell towers. [Chapter 1, Inner Planes]

Universal Law of Cause and Effect - The Universal Law of Cause and Effect states that whatever you send into the universe through your thoughts, words, or deeds comes back to you (karma). The Law of Cause and Effect is a way that the Universe or the Divine Mind attracts similar situations to you so that you can learn to make better choices. [Chapter 2, Increasing Spirituality]

About the Author

Jay Quinn has been an ordained minister since 1986 with the Spiritual Science Mother Church, established in 1923 in the State of New York. He joined the church Board in 2011 and has served as President of the Board since 2015.

Under the Spiritual Science Mother Church, Jay established a charter church called the Church of Angelic Grace in the State of Virginia in 2009. The mission of the Church of Angelic Grace is to foster spiritual growth through the application of healing principles and techniques.

Jay has been studying metaphysics for over 40 years and has a healing practice specializing in personal healing, intuitive counseling, energetic house and office clearings, and channeled messages and sacred symbols from the angelic realm. He is a trained kinesiologist and uses muscle testing to access the client's higher self and enlightened intelligences to balance physical, emotional, and mental issues. He is also an intuitive, a Buddhist practitioner, a shaman, an angelic facilitator, and a teacher. He has been formally teaching metaphysical classes since 2009. Jay has been guided by Spirit to do healing paintings that facilitate vibrational shifts on the soul level, and since January 2018, he has been channeling and teaching metaphysical techniques provided by Mary Magdalene to shift consciousness on an individual and global level. He holds healing study groups that meet twice a month on Saturdays in Alexandria, Virginia.

Jay was guided by Spirit to set up a publishing company called Higher Consciousness Press to print *The Teachings of Mary Magdalene* books as well as to make available his course materials of the classes listed below. The classes are available in downloadable PDF format for a reasonable fee.

Educational classes offered:

- Angelic Resonance® Healing Techniques©
- Angelic Resonance® Soul Symbols Class©
- Energetic Clearing & Balancing Workshop©
- Dealing with Non-Beneficial Energies© Workshop©
- Inner & Outer Teachings©
- Clearings for Prosperity Workshop for Realtors©
- The Twenty Wisdom Teachings©
- Universal Wisdom Reiki©
- Spiritual Reiki Teachings©
- Connective Awareness Process©
- Accessing Unconscious Information via Muscle Testing

For more information on *The Teachings of Mary Magdalene* series of books or for downloadable educational courses, visit either: naturalhealingoptions.com or higherconsciousnesspress.com.

You may also contact Jay Quinn directly by email at higherconsciousnesspress@aol.com

Higher Consciousness Press
Raising awareness through self mastery

www.higherconsciousnesspress.com

Special Offer

Private Session with the Author

Higher Consciousness Press offers a three-hour private session with the author at a thirty-three percent discount off his normal hourly rate. If you are interested in this personalized opportunity, you can make arrangements at higherconsciousnesspress.com. Once your order processes, a mutually agreeable time will be set up for your one-on-one session.

www.ingramcontent.com/pod-product-compliance
Lightning Source LLC
Chambersburg PA
CBHW042036100526
44587CB00030B/4444